Made in United States
North Haven, CT
21 December 2024

63201241R00057